NATIVE AMERICAN ART

ART HISTORY BOOKS FOR KIDS

Children's Art Books

BABY PROFESSOR
EDUCATION KIDS

Speedy Publishing LLC
40 E. Main St. #1156
Newark, DE 19711
www.speedypublishing.com

n this book, we're going to talk about Native American Art. So, let's get right to it!

There are over 5 hundred different Native American tribes in North America. Every tribe has a unique culture and this is reflected in their art, both past and present. Native American art spans thousands of years of history and includes beautiful beadwork, elaborate silver and turquoise jewelry, basketry and weaving. It also includes pottery, many different types of carvings, as well as kachinas, which are dolls representing spirit beings.

Native American Indian chief headdress with red pattern.

Carved masks and the musical instruments of drums, pipes, and flutes were used in their performance art, as were headdresses. Totem poles told their stories and showed their skill with carving wood.

Native American Drums with Rain Stick and Spirit Chaser.

Stanley Park Totem Pole Vancouver.

WHICH MATERIALS WERE USED IN THEIR ART?

Some of the earliest art created by Native Americans were cave paintings as well as earthenware and works made of stone that date back to thousands of years ago. Over the years, they used rocks and feathers to create art, and then in later periods, they used different types of cloth, glass, and clay. In their jewelry, turquoise and silver combinations have always been popular. Each piece of art reflects the different tribes of native people.

Pictographs Native American Indian.

CAVE PAINTINGS

In 2013, archaeologists discovered what they believe to be the oldest rock art in the United States. The images had been hidden for over 6,000 years. They were found in the Cumberland Plateau in the State of Tennessee. It's thought that this collection is the most widespread ever found in the United States. The pictures show scenes from hunts.

Some of the pictures show animals that lived alongside the Native Americans. They appear to have been drawn with some type of pointed tool. Not all the pictures were realistic scenes. Some of them were representative of spiritual beliefs and showed creatures that were part of the Native American myths.

Fremont rock art, ancient petroglyphs. Moab, Utah, USA.

This amazing find was discovered by four researchers in the Anthropology departments at Mississippi State and the University of Tennessee. Other notable rock painting discoveries in Tennessee are at Dunbar Cave and also at Mud Glyph Cave in the city of Clarksville.

Archaeologists and art historians believe that Native Americans drew rock paintings as part of their spiritual ceremonies. Preservation is important when these ancient treasures are discovered. The pictures are fragile because they were created in the mud. Mud was all around, especially in the southeast portion of the United States, and made a good canvas on the walls of a prehistoric cave.

In these ancient paintings, human beings are shown participating in ceremonies. Sometimes they are doing something heroic or something they would like to do, such as fly, transform into animals, or reach through rock walls.

A common theme in rock paintings, in addition to human forms, is to depict anthropomorphs. These are either animals or spiritual beings that are shown as humans. For example, a buffalo that was drawn walking like a human would be an anthropomorph. Sometimes anthropomorphs are shown with exaggerated features like huge ears, enormous horns, or large hands with extra-long fingers.

Sage stick and American Indian feathers.

THE CONNECTION BETWEEN SPIRITUALITY AND NATIVE AMERICAN ART

The Native American tribes have a deep spiritual connection with all of nature. The sun and the moon are frequent symbols in their art. Bears and eagles were two types of animals that were frequent subjects. Bears represented strength and courage. Eagles represented peaceful friendships. This deep tie to Mother Nature is apparent in almost all Native American art. Jewelry pendants as well as statues were created in honor of Mother Nature and the bounty she provided. Artists and craftspeople took the time to make even ordinary objects beautiful.

NATIVE AMERICAN TOTEM POLES

One of the types of art that most people immediately think of when they think of Native American art is the totem pole. Totem poles are sculptures that are carved from very large trees like the Western Red Cedar. Many of the native peoples in the Pacific Northwest and Alaska created totem poles.

In addition to being an amazing work of art, a totem pole tells a story or is a visual history of an important event. Each figure that is carved on the totem pole is part of the story or event. A totem records the story or history for future generations to remember. Unlike other cultures who used sculptures mostly to represent their gods, the Native American totem pole generally represents characteristics or traits of the particular tribe or clan of the story that's depicted.

Totem pole.

In addition to the story and history totem poles, there are other types of totem poles, too. A totem pole can be erected to show a line of ancestors in order to indicate the social standing of a family or tribe. Memorial poles have sometimes been erected to honor a deceased member of the tribe and some mortuary poles to honor the dead have a place inside for the dead person's ashes.

One of the most unusual types of poles is a pole that shames a person in order to make a public statement of whatever it is that the person did wrong. After the shamed person makes the appropriate amends, the totem pole is taken down.

Most totem poles were painted with black, red, or blue-green since these were the colors available from natural materials. Black was made with graphite or with charcoal. Red came from a clay-like substance called ochre. Blue-green was made into a pigment using copper sulfide.

Totem pole.

The raven symbolizes the Creator so it is often shown on totem poles. Other common subjects are eagles, which represent friendship and peace. The thunderbird, a mythical bird with mysterious powers, is a common theme on totems and other Native American art. Beavers, bears, wolves, and frogs are carved on totems too.

Totem wood pole .

The importance of the figure had nothing to do with where it was located on the totem pole. The most important figure could have been at the top, middle, or bottom.

Totem poles have been part of the history of Native American art for centuries and are still created today.

Totem pole in North America.

Collection of Native American Turquoise and Silver Jewelry.

NATIVE AMERICAN JEWELRY

Jewelry created by Native American artists is rich with symbolism from nature and their enduring legends. It's used for many reasons. One reason is simply decorative. Another is to protect. A third reason is to honor. A fourth reason was to show the social class of the individual wearing it. Native American jewelry is sought after by collectors for its elaborate designs and intricate patterns. Most of the inspiration for the jewelry comes from the natural world.

As well as the commonly used silver and turquoise, one of the other materials used was copper.

Copper was used before the Europeans introduced the Native Americans to silversmithing. They also used gemstones such as opal and onyx. Europeans also introduced glass beads, which the Native Americans used to create new types of beaded jewelry.

Native American artifacts.

Dream Catchers.

THE OJIBWE
DREAMCATCHER

A completely unique form of art that was created by Native Americans in the Southwest is the dreamcatcher. The Ojibwe tribe created this interesting form of art that looks something like a net that's hung sideways with adornments of feathers or beads on it. The dreamcatcher has a spiritual meaning.

The holes are thought to filter out negative feelings. It was sometimes hung to help children avoid nightmares at night. Dreamcatchers have become very popular and have inspired jewelry designs as well as other art forms.

Dreamcatcher for sweet dreams.

Navajo Wedding Baskets.

NAVAJO RUG WEAVING AND SAND PAINTING

The weaving of blankets and rugs is another beautiful form of art in which the Native Americans excel. Women would spend hundreds of hours to make the intricate rainbows of patterns and elaborate designs used in the blankets and rugs.

The Navajo have a legend that the Spider Woman created the fabric of the universe and when she was finished, she taught her secrets of weaving to the Navajo tribe. It is a tradition that has been passed down through hundreds of years through the generations.

Navajo weaving.

The sand paintings are created in the mornings as well as the early afternoons in the final days of a sacred ceremony. The ceremony will be conducted by the medicine man and his assistants. After the ceremony, the beautiful one-of-a-kind piece is dismantled.

Old Native American Pima and Papago baskets

The subject matter and the designs of sand paintings are transferred from generation to generation by memory. This form of art is sacred and symbolic. To the Navajo people it represents the arrival of their gods and heroes.

Awesome! Now you know more about the works of Native American artists. You can find more Art books from Baby Professor by searching the website of your favorite book retailer.

Visit

BABY PROFESSOR
EDUCATION KIDS

www.BabyProfessorBooks.com

to download Free Baby Professor eBooks
and view our catalog of new and exciting
Children's Books

Made in the USA
Coppell, TX
17 July 2020